Sum...
of

The Girl with Seven Names
Lee Hyeon Seo

Conversation Starters

By BookHabits

Tips for Using BookHabits Conversation Starters:

EVERY GOOD BOOK CONTAINS A WORLD FAR DEEPER THAN the surface of its pages. The characters and their world come alive through the words on the pages, yet the characters and its world still live on. Questions herein are designed to bring us beneath the surface of the page and invite us into the world that lives on. These questions can be used to:

- Foster a deeper understanding of the book
- Promote an atmosphere of discussion for groups
- Assist in the study of the book, either individually or corporately
- Explore unseen realms of the book as never seen before

About Us:

THROUGH YEARS OF EXPERIENCE AND FIELD EXPERTISE, from newspaper featured book clubs to local library chapters, *BookHabits* can bring your book discussion to life. Host your book party as we discuss some of today's most widely read books.

Table of Contents

Introducing *The Girl with Seven Names*

"The Girl with Seven Names" was published in 2015. It was written by Lee Hyeon-seo. The book is her story of escape, or defection, from North Korea. The story begins before her time, with a little bit of backstory about her birth parents, and then the man who eventually becomes her father. Her story begins in January of 1980, in Hyesan, North Korea. She is named Kim Ji-hae, and this is the first of her seven names. Her second name, Park Min-young, is given to her after her mother's second marriage. This is both to save her from being given to another family, and to secure her place in society.

Her brother is brought into the story when she is seven years old. This is also the age at which she witnesses her first public hanging. North Korea is a harsh world to live in, and the hanging is her first glimpse of the cruelty surrounding her. The story then goes on to detail her school years, during which North Korea's Great Leader, Kim Il-sung dies. The furor caused by his death clues her in to just how rigid the system really is in North Korea.

At the age of seventeen, Min-young as she is known by at that time, takes off across the Yalu River to China. She expects to spend a very short amount of time there, then come back into North Korea to attend university once she turns eighteen. But, her visit to China changes her life, forever.

She cannot go back home to North Korea. Her mother has reported her missing, and she is now an illegal alien hiding in China. She may have more freedom than she did in North Korea, but her life is now a big question mark. While staying with her aunt and uncle in Shenyang, she is introduced to a whole new world. To secure her safety while in China, she must once more change her name. Her third name is Chae Mi-ran, and she must learn Mandarin to survive. The feelings of guilt and abandonment of her mother and brother cause her to have nightmares, and this causes her relatives to become concerned for her.

They introduce her to a young man named Jang Geun-soo. The two, young people go out here and there, and she is introduced to his mother. Mrs. Jang starts dictating Mi-ran's life, and she is expected to marry Geun-soo. He even shows her the new identification badge they have for her when they marry. Her fourth name would be Jang Soon-hyang. She cannot handle the feeling she is losing her freedom once again to marriage, so she leaves and strikes out on her own.

She heads to Xita, China, which is Shenyang's version of Koreatown. She figures she will be able to find a job there. Upon arriving in the city, she is almost immediately approached by a woman names Miss Ma, who offers her a job. Thinking she has happened upon good fortune, she goes with the woman. They end up at a men's hair salon, but it's not the job she thought she would be doing. She learns she is to be an escort and a prostitute. She runs once again.

She eventually finds herself a job as a waitress. While working in a Koreatown restaurant, she is picked up by the police and questioned extensively in Mandarin. She is grateful she learned to read, write, and speak the language well. Her knowledge of Mandarin grants her freedom. However, just a short time after the interrogation, she is attacked and left for dead. Though she survives the attack, it makes her wary once again, to the point she no longer trusts anyone around her.

It is winter of 2001. She is lonely and distracted, and she misses her family. She contacts a Chinese broker to help her find her family in North Korea. This is what she thinks of as Plan B. Plan A consists of contacting the Ahn family who helped her travel to her aunt and uncle's house upon arrival in China. Mrs. Ahn agrees to try to contact Min-ho and set up a possible meeting with him. Less than one month later, Mrs. Ahn contacts her via telephone, and she meets up with and talks to her brother for the first time in years. He is now a young man, not a little boy any longer.

The Chinese broker shows up at the Ahn house while she is there, claiming to also have found her family. To meet with them, she would have to pay them a large fee. Though she knows this is a lie, she leaves with them to ensure her brother's safety. She is held for four days before she can secure arrangements to pay the men. Miraculously, she is not harmed during this time. Once they let her go, she runs for her life to Shanghai. She once again changes her name to try to keep herself safe. Her fifth name is Chae In-hee.

Though she has run to Shanghai, she is still lonely and missing her family. She purchases an identification tag, causing her to take a sixth name: Park Sun-ja. It is now 2003. Sun-ja receives an out-of-the-blue phone call from her brother, asking for money and a cellphone. She quickly agrees. This leads to routine phone calls between Sun-ja and her family, and this leads her to act on her longing to have them reunite after so long. Approximately one year later, she learns North Korean defectors can seek asylum in South Korea. She starts planning to move to Seoul, and to get her family there as well.

Finally, in January 2008, she purchases her airline ticket to South Korea. Once in South Korea, she tells officials there she is seeking asylum from North Korea. But, because of her clothing and her name-brand luggage, she isn't believed at first. Eventually she is taken to a processing center and put into a large room with an assortment of other women. She is interrogated fully and subsequently sent to Hanowon.

Hanowon is the place defectors are sent to learn how to live in South Korea. They are there for approximately two months, and they either acclimate themselves to their new lives – or they don't. Many simply cannot and are sent back to North Korea. The remaining defectors are then sent to a city of the government's choosing to start their new lives. She was sent to Seoul. It is nearing the end of 2008, and she must decide how to proceed with her new life, as well as her reunion plans. She is thirty years old.

She once again changes her name, but this time she chooses her new name. Her seventh, and final name, will be Lee Hyeon-seo. Hyeon means sunshine, and Seo means good fortune. She gives herself the best new start she can and applies to local universities with her new name. Eventually, through many more struggles, she finally brings her mother and brother to Seoul. She meets the man of her dreams (an American), and later marries him. She attends and graduates from university. She also becomes a proud international speaker against the tribulations of residing in North Korea, helping others to defect and live their lives more freely in South Korea. Finally, she is free, and she is happy.

Discussion Questions

"Get Ready to Enter a New World"

Tip: Begin with questions dealing with broader issues to ensure ample time for quality discussions. Read through all discussion questions before engaging.

~~~

question 1

Compare the government types between the
United States and North Korea.

~~~

question 2

Hyeon-seo's "punishment" for disobeying her mother was she could never come back home, though it was for her safety and theirs. How does that differ from punishment's given to teenage girls today who may choose to leave their homes? Explain.

~~~

~ ~ ~

question 3

Hyeon-seo did not learn about sexual intercourse until she accidentally saw a pornographic movie at a friend's home. She did not learn about lesbianism until she was placed into a women's prison. Young people today learn about these things at much younger ages, which sometimes leads to pregnancy or other issues. Is it better for children today to be aware of sex and sexual issues, or to be ignorant where these things are concerned? Explain.

~ ~ ~

~~~

question 4

Religion is a very controversial subject today. In North Korea, religion is forbidden. The only way to worship is to worship the country's leader. Are there any other countries today which forbid religion? Explain.

~~~

question 5

The book makes it obvious Hyeon-seo's journey was harrowing. Yet, she chose to share her story with the world. Was she brave or unwise to share her story? Explain.

~~~

question 6

From the beginning of her story, Hyeon-seo has portrayed herself as headstrong or stubborn, sometimes more than she should be. There are several instances of this: wanting to wear fashionable clothing rather than a uniform, not mourning the death of the country's leader, and running away from home. Hoe does her stubbornness aide her while she is trying to survive in China? Explain.

~~~

~~~

question 7

Hyeon-seo spends over a decade attempting to bring her mother and brother to the "safety" of South Korea. She is eventually reunited with them. How often do people today spend over a decade trying to reach or obtain a specific goal? Is this rare or common? Explain.

~~~

~~~

question 8

While living with her aunt and uncle, Hyeon-seo is introduced to a young man. After going on a few dates and meeting the young man's mother, she is then expected to marry him. She ends up running away from the situation. Arranged marriages are quite common in North Korea, as well as in a few other countries, though not in the United States. What is another custom which is prevalent elsewhere, but not practiced in the United States? Explain.

~~~

~~~

question 9

Hyeon-seo learned at the age of twelve her father was not her birth father. This caused issues in the relationships between Hyeon-seo, her "father", and her little brother. The death of her father brought the siblings closer once again. Does death always bring family together? Why or why not?

~~~

~~~

question 10

Finding out she was adopted was quite a shock for Hyeon-seo. Should parents tell their children they were adopted or not? Explain.

~~~

~ ~ ~

question 11

Hyeon-seo began having nightmares after settling in with her aunt and uncle in China? Can guilt and depression be the cause of nightmares? Why or why not? What are other negative outcomes of guilt and depression?

~ ~ ~

~~~

question 12

Once in China, Hyeon-seo is told she must learn Mandarin to survive there. She starts by using children's books and watching Chinese television shows. Eventually she can read, write, and speak Mandarin fluently. How difficult is learning another language well enough to speak it fluently? Does stress make learning easier or more difficult? Why or why not?

~~~

~~~

question 13

Because her father was in the air force, Hyeon-seo and her family moved quite a bit. After leaving North Korea, Hyeon-seo was once again forced to stay on the move. Did the moving while she was young help or hinder her once she was in China? How difficult is it for a family to move repeatedly versus a single person? Explain.

~~~

question 14

Songbun is the North Korean caste system. This word means the family is in good standing, or elite, within the community. Bowibu is the North Korean military or special police. What would the equivalents of the words be in the United States? Explain.

~ ~ ~

question 15

Hyeon-seo changed her name a total of seven times. How difficult is it to change one's name in the United States? Explain the process.

~ ~ ~

question 16

Fellow author, Jang Jin-sung, feels Hyeon-seo's story is "sad and beautiful". In which ways can the story be considered sad? Beautiful? Explain.

~~~

~~~

question 17

Many reviewers have used a plethora of adjectives to leave their opinion of Hyeon-seo's story: brave, riveting, and committed were just a few. Which one adjective sums up her story the best? Why or how?

~~~

~~~

question 18

One reviewer refers to the story as "heartbreaking". Yet, ultimately, Hyeon-seo is triumphant and happy at the end of the story. How can the story be both heartbreaking and happy at the same time? Explain.

~~~

~~~

question 19

One review makes a point to mention this book is simply one of many recently released which were written by defectors from North Korea. While each book or story is individual, the horror each escaped is the same. How is writing a book about their defection a way to help release and lessen the horrors each of these authors faced? Explain.

~~~

question 20

One reviewer claims the story trades on the truth that freedom is complicated. What does this mean exactly? Is this a valid point? Why or why not?

~~~

Introducing the Author

Lee Hyeon-Seo was born in Hyesan, North Korea, in 1980. However, this was not the name she was given at birth. The name she was given at birth was Kim Ji-hae, and her name would change a total of seven times during her early life.

Ji-hae's parents did not have a normal marriage. Her birth father was an official from Pyongyang, and her mother was from a well-to-do family. Though her mother was in love with another man, she was made to marry this official by her own mother to save face and their good standing in the community. The marriage lasted just over one year, and Ji-hae was the only good result of the marriage. Her parents never even lived together.

Divorce was frowned upon, as was being a single mother. Ji-hae's grandmother wanted her to be put up for adoption, but her mother refused. She went looking for the soldier she had fallen in love with, and found him on base. The two reconnected, married, and Ji-hae was adopted as this man's daughter.

Because the marriage and adoption needed to be successful, Ji-hae's name was changed to Park Min-young. She was four years old at the time. Her little brother, Min-ho, arrived when she was seven years old. He, too, was born in Hyesan. Min-young did not find out her "father" wasn't truly her birth father until she was approximately twelve years old. This caused a huge crack in the relationships she had with him and with her little brother.

Her father stopped working for the air force shortly after she learned the truth about her parentage. He started working for a North Korean trading company. The job took him in and out of the country often, which caused great stress for her mother. When Min-young was fourteen years old, her father was arrested at the border coming back into North Korea from China. He was jailed for approximately two weeks before being sent to a hospital. He never recovered from the situation, and subsequently died in the hospital from an overdose. The children never got to say goodbye to him. The unfortunate incident helped Min-young and Min-ho repair their sibling relationship.

North Korea is a very strict and forbidding country to grow up in. Min-young, like all other children in North Korea, grew up idolizing the country's leaders, Kim Il-sung and Kim Jong-il. Father and son, they were referred to as the Great Leader and the Dear Leader respectively. Every home was required to keep a portrait of each man in a respected spot. Inspections were done routinely to ensure the portraits were clean and being taken care of properly. During a devastating house fire, the only thing saved from Min-young's home was the two portraits of the country's leaders.

Min-young's schooling was geared towards teaching the children North Korea's truths about their wonderful leaders and their wonderful country. All other countries were said to be horrible and the cause of major problems according to their teachers. The whole country went into shock when Kim Il-sung died in 1994. It was required that all citizens, adults and children alike, were to mourn his death. If one did not mourn him properly, he or she was put to death.

Striving for a tiny bit of freedom before her eighteenth birthday, Min-young wanted to cross the Yalu River into China. Her country was becoming a land of famine, starvation and death under Kim Jong-il's rule. Approximately one month before her eighteenth birthday, defying her mother, Min-young stole away to China. She was unaware at the time that it would be almost twelve years before she would see her mother again.

Once in China, Min-young travelled to her aunt and uncle's home in Shenyang. They took her in and helped her, causing her short stay to become longer than expected as she was enjoying her freedom immensely. Approximately one month after she travelled to China, Min-young received a phone call from her mother telling her she couldn't come back home. This changed her life forever.

Over the next decade or so, Min-young changed her name numerous times to ensure her safety. She eventually made her way to South Korea to seek asylum there as a defector. She further struggled to bring her mother and brother to South Korea as well. Once she made a home for herself in Seoul, South Korea, she was able to legally change her name to one of her choice: Lee Hyeon-seo.

With help from assorted people, working an assortment of jobs, she was finally reunited with her family. Hyeon-seo put herself through university, and today is an avid speaker and aide to others looking to defect and seek asylum away from North Korea. She is happily married to an American man, and lives in Seoul, South Korea.

Fireside Questions

"What would you do?"

Tip: These questions can be a fun exercise as it spurs creativity among the readers by allowing alternate scene endings and "if this was you" questions.

question 21

Though she had planned to attend university once she turned eighteen, Hyeon-seo's life took a drastic turn instead. She did eventually attend and graduate from university, but she was in her thirties. Does age affect one's learning? Why or why not?

~~~

~~~

question 22

In 2013, Hyeon-seo gave a TED talk, telling her story for the first time. She published her story in 2015. How important was it for her story to be told? Explain.

~~~

~~~

question 23

Hyeon-seo saw a public hanging for the first time at the age of seven. When hangings were scheduled, everyone was required to attend and watch. What kind of damage could this do to a child? Explain.

~~~

~~~

question 24

Hyeon-seo was taught in school to be aware of all other countries. North Korea was the best country, and all others were terrible, horrible places. Yet, she married an American man. What does this say for her mindset, acknowledging how she was taught and raised? Is this a positive or a negative, considering how many issues there are today surrounding interracial relationships and marriages? Explain.

~~~

~ ~ ~

question 25

Hyeon-seo's grandmother wanted Hyeon-seo's mother to give her up for adoption after her divorce. She refused to do so. Would a grandparent be able to force her child to give up their child for adoption today? Yes or no? If so, in what circumstances? Explain.

~ ~ ~

question 26

Every home in North Korea was required to hang portraits of the Great Leader and the Dear Leader. During a house fire, those portraits were the only items saved. All else was lost. Though it is not always possible to save anything from a house fire, portraits would not be the only thing a family in the United States would be likely to grab. Providing family members and pets are safe, what item would be important to save from a house fire is possible? Explain.

~~~

question 27

Hyeon-seo actively helps others to defect from North Korea. She also actively tries to raise awareness around the drastic conditions while living in North Korea. Step into her shoes. Would you do the same? Or would you stay as far away from anything having to do with North Korea as possible? Explain.

~~~

~~~

question 28

Hyeon-seo tells officials she is seeking asylum from North Korea when she lands at the airport in Incheon, South Korea. They do not believe her at first because she is dressed fashionable and has name brand luggage. What sort of feelings can be felt when one is speaking the truth but is not believed? Explain.

~~~

~~~

question 29

When the Great Leader died, the entire country was expected to mourn. If one didn't mourn properly, he or she was publicly executed. What would the difference be if the President of the United States were to die unexpectedly?

~~~

~~~

question 30

This young lady started this harrowing journey at the age of seventeen. Is there anyone you know personally who could have made the same journey at the age of seventeen? Explain.

~~~

Quiz Questions

"Ready to Announce the Winners?"

Tip: Create a leaderboard and track scores to see who gets the most correct answers. Winners required. Prizes optional.

~~~

quiz question 1

True or False: Hyeon-seo chose to stay in China, causing her not to be able to go back home.

~~~

~ ~ ~

quiz question 2

"The Girl with Seven Names" was published in
_____.

~ ~ ~

~~~

quiz question 3

True or False: Hyeon-seo's little brother was named Min-ho.

~~~

~~~

quiz question 4

Hyeon-seo's aunt and uncle lived in
_____, China.

~~~

~ ~ ~

quiz question 5

True or False: One of the jobs Hyeon-seo took to support herself was as an escort.

~ ~ ~

~ ~ ~

quiz question 6

Hyeon-seo purchased her ticket to Seoul in

_____.

~ ~ ~

~~~

quiz question 7

True or False: Hyeon-seo never reunited with her mother and brother.

~~~

~ ~ ~

quiz question 8

Hyeon-seo's given name at birth was
_____.

~ ~ ~

quiz question 9

True or False: Hyeon-seo was eighteen when crossed the Yalu River into China.

~~~

~~~

quiz question 10

Hyeon-seo was born in _____, North Korea.

~~~

~~~

quiz question 11

True or False: Hyeon-seo Lee married a man from Seoul, South Korea.

~~~

quiz question 12

After Hyeon-seo was held for four days by the men of a Chinese broker, she packed up and moved to _____.

Quiz Answers

1. True
2. 2015
3. True
4. Shenyang
5. False
6. January 2008
7. False
8. Kim Ji-hae
9. False
10. Hyesan
11. False
12. Shanghai

Ways to Continue Your Reading

EVERY month, our team runs through a wide selection of books to pick the best titles for readers and reading groups, and promotes these titles to our thousands of readers – sometimes with free downloads, sale dates, and additional brochures.

If you have not yet read the original work or would like to read it again, get the book here.

Want to register yourself or a book group? It's free and takes 1-click.

Register here.

On the Next Page...

Please write us your reviews! Any length would be fine but we'd appreciate hearing you more! We'd be SO grateful.

Till next time,

BookHabits

"Loving Books is Actually a Habit"